INSIGHT PUBLICA®

INSIGHT PUBLICA

Kozhikode, Kerala, India 673011
www.insightpublica.com
e-mail: insightpublica@gmail.com
The Mysterious Forest
Cinasha
First Insight Publica Edition: December 2020

ISBN 978-93-90535-24-8
Cover Painting & Drawings: Cinasha

THE MYSTERIOUS FOREST

Cinasha

INSIGHT PUBLICA®

CINASHA

Cinasha studying in eighth standard at Government Higher secondary School Kasaragod in Kerala. She was born on 29th October 2007 to Sreekumar and Smitha. Cinasha is interested in reading drawing and writing. Her two English novels 'The Mysterious Forest' and 'Song Of The River' were published on November 2019. She wrote these novels when she was studying in 6th standard.

Address: Cinasha, D/o Sreekumar A, Maipady (PO)
Kasaragod, Kerala, Pin : 671124
Ph: 9497842169, email: sreekumar2515@gmail.com

An Interesting Narrative

This novel is an interesting narrative representation by a eleven years old girl in writing and drawing... not a novel published after an appraisal by an editor's eye but published as a support for a young mind's interest and exploration. As her interest and exploration cannot be confined to the prison house of grammar, we have let her free of those syntactic shackles. We welcome you readers to this book so syntactically free and imaginatively rich. You won't be disappointed in reading it.

Sumesh Insight

CONTENTS

Chapter One

SIX BEST FRIENDS

"Let's come-up to a gang!" said Arid George hopefully to Cini. "What? A GANG?" Cini looked surprised

"Yes, a gang! What's your opinion?" asked Oard.

"Well - I am ready! Let's make-up a gang. All right, Muppu?"

Cini was happy.

So Arid, Oard and the other two boys looked at Mufaza.

"Yes, Cinu, Why not?"

She was glad, too.

"Woo-hoo..! so we are a gang!" Weron jumped in joy.

"What is the name of our gang?"

asked Aman.

"Mmmm..... Super Six!" Arid said.

"Let's name our best friends gang super six!" "Of course!" everyone agreed.

That was the beginning of their sweet friendship. Cini had been studying in that same school since 1st grade. Aman, Weron and Oard, too. Cini's petname was Cinu, Aman's Amu, Weron's Wern and Oard's Oye. Arid came to that school this year. Mufaza came to the school in this year, too. She was called Muppu. Now they are in the 6th. Now they are BEST FRIENDS and Super Six Gang.

One day two teachers were off, and the naughty children of 6th were, not minding the bell and playing outside in the ground in the ENGLISH PERIOD.

It's a jolly day because the child named Muron didn't come to school. He was the main enemy of Super Six because he tried to break their friendship.

So, it was a happy day. There, girls were playing a game named chasing and catching. Suddenly Wern came there.

"Hey - Cinu and Muppu; come to play football". He called.

"What a joke, Girls playing FOOTBALL! Ha, ha, ha! Hey, go away, boy!" the other girls laughed.

"I am not talking to YOU!" Wern went red.

“Ok, ok! I am coming. Let’s go, Muppu.” said Cinu.

“Yes. Hey, Girls Gang..... We are leaving” said Muppu to the other girls. They were called Girls Gang. So Wern, Muppu and Cinu went to the football ground. There, Oye, Arid, Aman and some other boys were waiting with a football.

They split into two teams. Super Six and some other boys were in one team. All others were in another team, suddenly Muppu said : “I am not playing!”

“Why?” asked Cinu.

“I don’t know how to play football!”

“Oh.. don’t mind that! Girls in Super Six are SMART!”

Cinu tried to give her courage.

“So, come on!”

At last, Muppu did set on the ground and now they’re getting ready to play.

Suddenly Aman asked “What would be our team’s and their team’s name?”

Hearing this, the captain of the other team Deensh said suddenly;

“My team is BRAZIL!” Everybody knew that he was a Brazil fan.

“No, no. Our team is PORTUGAL!” Shirag, another player of that team said.

“Yes, Portugal-Portugal.” Other Portugal fans in that team agreed to Shirag.”

“Ok, the team is Portugal.”

said Deensh, a little disappointed.

“So what’s our team, Cinu?”

Arid asked to Cinu. “Well-without a doubt, we are ARGENTINA!” Cinu smiled. She and Arid were Argentina fans. So, they started the game. Muppu scored a goal. So, the game ended and Argentina won (1-0).

“Hurray....!” all six jumped up in joy.

Suddenly Aman said as he remembered some shocking thing:

“Hey, it’s MATHS PERIOD!”

Everyone became shocked. They had forgotten all about the time while playing.

“Oh- I think Prisa miss will be in the class.” Cinu said worried.

Prisa was their Maths teacher who was very very strict.

"Hey guys, let's go!"

All ran to the class room.

They reached the classroom. There were other girls standing outside the classroom. They saw Prisa miss with a stick. She was very angry. Everyone pushed each other but no one dared to ask, 'may I come in teacher.'

At last, Wern asked, “May I come in, teacher?” Prisa came to them.

“Where were you all this time?”

She thundered. No one answered.

“You can’t sit in my class today!”

She thundered again.

“Get out!”

All stood there. Now all children of 6th were out and Prisa went to the staff room.

Then children started to talk.

“This does not matter. The main thing is we won the game!”

Super six laughed

Chapter Two

JICKY

Cinu was doing her homework on her study-table. Her mother was talking on the phone to Aunt Shini. Cinu could hear her mother's words:

"Hi...."

"Oh, you are going to some new place for business."

"When will you come back?"

"Many months?"

"Oh.. then Jicky?"

"Jicky here?"

"Hmm mm, Cinu would be so glad!"

"Ok, bye!"

She cut the phone and turned to Cinu. "Mum, What's that talk about Jack?"

Cinu called Jicky, "Jack" as she calls her dearest friends nicknames.

"There's good news for you. Your Aunt Shini and Uncle John are going to some far away places for business duties.

You know, their son and daughter-your eldest cousins-are not in the house, they are in the hostels. So you know, your Granny went to Aunt Molly's house.

So, Jicky will be alone in the house. They are bringing Jicky here!" mother said with a smile.

"Woo-Hoo! Jack is coming here..! and she will stay here for MONTHS! I really love it..." Cinu danced in joy.

Jicky was a German Shepherd dog, the pet in Aunt Shini's house. There lived Granma, Aunt Shini, Uncle John and their son and daughter. Now Granma is in Aunt Moly's house. Aunt and Uncle will leave, so the children are in hostels.

Cinu and Jicky were good friends. Now she will come to her house. Cinu loved dogs.

A Couple of days later, in the evening Cinu and Arid were going back to their houses from school as they were neighbours. "Hey Cinu, a big dog is there in front of your house! There is a wooden Kennel, too!"

Arid was very surprised. Cinu looked at there eagerly. There is Jicky! Cinu jumped up in joy.

Jicky started barking loudly to see a new boy. Arid was scared to see a big German Shepherd barking at him.

"Jicky...! Hey my jack..."

Cinu ran down to Jicky. Jicky suddenly stopped barking and licked her feet in love.

Arid looked more SURPRISED.

"Arid, this is Jack-I mean Jicky. She was in my Granny's house. Now everyone in that house had gone to some other places for business purposes. So she will live here for months. Don't be scared she will be friendly with you soon." Cinu looked at Arid.

"Ok, now, bye"

Arid went to his house. He lives there with his Uncle, Aunt and elder cousins Anna & Anny.

Then Cinu's mum came. "Oh, there you are...! Your Aunt and Uncle came herewith Jicky in the car. At noon, they left. They brought her kennel too" she said. But Cinu was hearing nothing. She was playing with Jicky, very very happily.

Chapter Three

ON THE WILD PATH

It was a hot day. Cinu had been talking only about Jicky to her friends. It was friday, and their lunch-break in school is very long.

Super Six were in the ground, trying to create a new game. "Let's play a RUNNING game." Suggested Wern.

"And we'll split into two teams. One team will be the runners and another team will be the chasers." said Cinu.

"Chasers team will count to 50 in the classroom." said Aman.

"By that time, runners will run" said Oye.

"And they can run or hide ANYWHERE they like."

"But can't in any building." Arid nodded. "And chasers will chase and catch them. If they catch everyone, runners will change into chasers and the chasers will change into runners and will continue the game." said Muppu.

"Hurry, now we made up a new game!"

"Girls are one team, boys are one team" said Oye.

So, Muppu and Cinu were in one team and Wern, Oye, Arid and Aman were the other team.

At first, Boys' team were chasers and Girls' team were runners. So, boys went to the class room and started counting. The girls ran away. Muppu and Cinu were running as fast as they could.

The boys finished counting and chased them. Cinu and Muppu ran in two different ways in a hurry. Cinu ran fast and reached the playground.

She looked back to see if the boys were coming. But

no one was coming. So, she took rest, sitting down in front of the classroom of high-schoolers. Suddenly she saw someone coming up. They were the BOYS! Cinu quickly ran and hid herself behind the classroom and listened, to what they were talking about.

"We caught Muppu! Only Cinu is left now!" said Wern.

"Yes, yes, we have to find and catch her!" said Aman.

Cinu suddenly saw, a LIZARD climbing on to her shoulders.

"Aaaooo..! "she forgot all about the game for a moment and cried aloud. Boys heard it. They found her.

"Hey, there is Cinu! Come on!" they ran towards Cinu.

"Aaahh...." Cinu dropped the lizard down and ran away, faster. She reached the green place where the mango tree stood. There the school compound ended. She needed to find a WAY.

Suddenly Cinu remembered the mysterious wild path. When she was in the 5th, she had found out a wild path starting from there and leading to somewhere. She was very interested about it but, her friends at that time didn't let her go and find the place where it ends. So, Cinu had to forget about it.

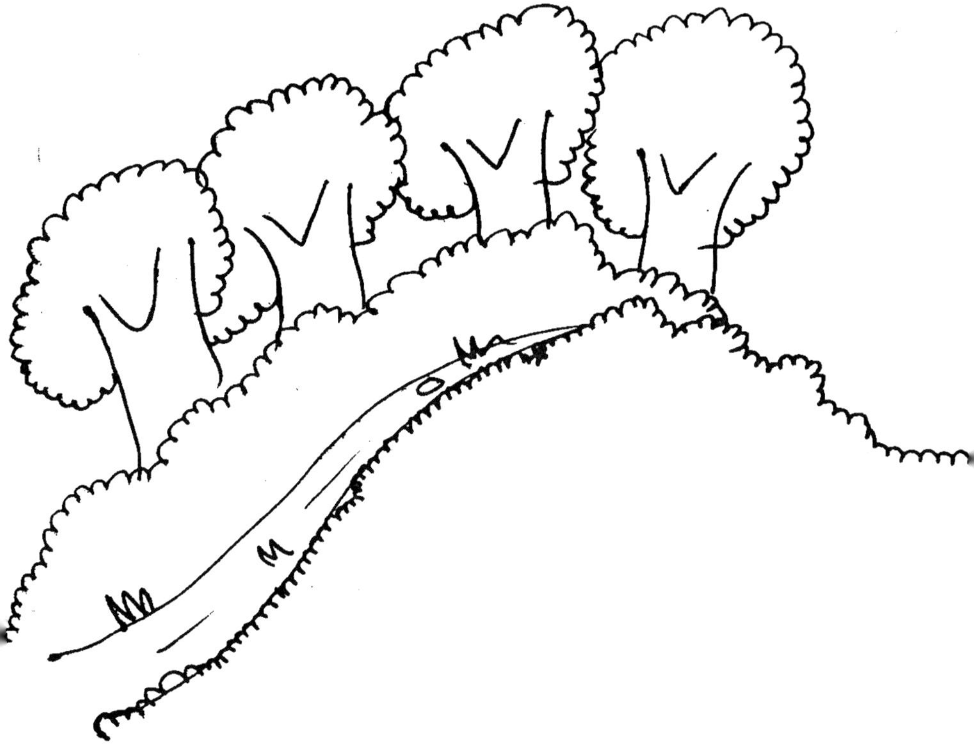

Now it's a good chance. The boys are coming. Cinu ran to the wild path. She suddenly stopped. She was very confused. One minute! She kept all adventure stories in her mind and ran through the path! Cinu ran and ran and finally the path ended. She was very tired and sat down on the grass, panting.

And when she got her breathe, she stood up there and looked around. It looked like a FOREST - A MYSTERIOUS one! There was a tiny, most wild path which looked like leading deep into the forest.

Cinu was really wonderstruck and asked herself, "AM I DREAMING?"

Chapter Four

IN THE FOREST

Cinu stood up. She asked herself. 'I have heard that pigs are living somewhere here! So can't I go?' She thought for a while. 'This is the best chance. This forest looks very mysterious and wonderful. I am sure that there are exciting wonders and mysteries to solve. Let me go and see it!'

Cinu was walking through the wild path. There was so many green trees not letting most of the sunlight come down and it's a bit dark there.

She walked, jumping over the rocks and fallen branches of trees. At last, she reached a place that exactly looked like a forest.

There were many many birds flying all around and singing on the trees. Green, green everywhere! “Wow!” Cinu wondered. She was very excited.

Chapter Five

A MYSTERIOUS MAN!

Cinu walked around that place curiously. Suddenly, she heard a noise like some one coming through the green bushes. 'Maybe the boys? But they wouldnot dare to come here!' She thought.

Is some one coming? Hurry! Cinu quickly tried to hide herself behind a tree, but she couldn't because there were a lot of ants. She saw a big beefy man there!

He was holding a backpack. He suddenly stopped to see a little girl there in front of him. Cinu was too surprised to see a big man there in front of her.

"HEY....!" the man cried.

"Ouch...."

Cinu gave a good run! She ran as fast as she could without looking back. Cinu ran faster and reached the place where the tiny path started.

Cinu ran and ran thinking 'who was that.' Finally she reached the mango tree area.

'Oh, where are my friends?'

Chapter Six

A DREAM OR NOT?

Cinu ran to the playground. There she saw, Muppu, Oye, Arid, Wern and Aman sitting on the step of the classroom. Wern said :

“Oh, where she is ? We searched

every where!”

“Hey - I am HERE!” Cinu called. Everyone looked.

“Cinu...!” the five went to her.

“Where’s your hiding place?” they asked eagerly.

“Ihave a big story to tell you!” Cinu said.

“So, what is it?” Everyone were interested.

“I was there behind the classroom first” she said.

“Yes, we saw it. But what after that?”

"I ran to the mango tree area and then I remembered about the mysterious wild path." "Remembered about the WHAT?"

"THE MYSTERIOUS WILD PATH!"

"What is it?"

Well let me explain. When I was in 5th I found a mysterious wild path starting from the mango tree area and leading to somewhere. And"

"Did you go through it then?"

"Not then. But in our game. I ran through it. And I reached a forest. Then there's - then there's A MAN!"

"Who was he? What he was doing there?" "I don't know. And he saw me.

I ran back to here" Cinu stopped.

Everyone were very very surprised.

"Cinu, do you mean, you got in a forest out and away from the school compound and saw a man there?" asked Wern.

"Yes!" Cinu nodded.

"Let's tell everything to the teacher." Muppu hurried.

"No, wait!" Others said.

"Teachers will ask us why she went out of the compound. And they will not believe us."

"And, what if she dreamed it all?" Arid said.

"No! I am SURE!" said Cinu.

“Ok, did you sit or take rest somewhere on the way?” everyone asked.

“Well-yes I did” said Cinu thinking about the place where the mysterious wild path ends.

“So, then you fell asleep and dreamed it all!”

“But, then my run?”

“Well, you saw the man in your dream and woke up and in the hurry and fear, ran!”

Five explained to Cinu.

“Maybe... Then I dreamed it all?” Cinu was now confused.

“Let’s keep this as a secret now. And let’s bring Jicky here next week and check what’s there.” Cinu said.

“But how?”

“You know, we have a residential camp for two weeks in our school starting next week. Then my mum will go to my aunt Sofi’s house. My father will be here. So we can secretly take Jack here!" Cinu explained.

Her father was a teacher in their school.

"Well-ok."

They, six went back to the classroom.

Chapter Seven

A TRICK!

One week passed. It was the first day of the camp. Cinu's mother went to aunt Sofiya's house. She had said that dad would come to the house every evening and give Jicky food and would put food for the time until the next evening. The super six had made a plan, already.

Everyone reached the school in the morning. Cinu was looking for her friends. Suddenly her dad - as a teacher - came and said it was time for everyone to assemble in the school auditorium. So she went there. There she sat on a chair looking for the other five among many students.

Suddenly she got a tap and a friendly soft punch on her head and she looked back; there was Muppu, Arid, Aman , Oye and Wern standing right behind her with a little smile.

"Oh, you sit here!" Cinu pointed to the empty chairs near her. Everyone sat down.

"Is everything ok?" asked Arid.

"I think so. I didn't take my pen like we planned" Cinu said.

"SILENCE!" said Prisa aloud and the auditorium fell silent.

Then there was the speech of a teacher about the camp. The camp was about 14 days. The first 4 days are for Education games. Next 4 days are for seeing good world films for children. Next 4 days are for sports. The last 2 days are for writing.

After the meeting, children had a break. Then the six went to the class teacher - Cinu's dad and she asked, "I forgot to take my pen! Can I go to home and take the pen?"

Her house was very near to the school.

"Hmmm, come back fast." He gave permission.

Six looked at each other and smiled.

Suddenly Cinu said, "Um. I will arrange food for Jicky for one or two weeks!"

"Why?" teacher asked.

"So, you don't have to go home everyday and put food for her. It's easy for you..." She said.

"OK" he agreed.

On the way to Cinu's house. Muppu asked. "Why did you say that will arrange food?"

"That's because, we are going to bring Jack. So, if my dad goes to the house to give food to her, he will know that she is not there. So I told him I would give her food and put more for two weeks. So he won't come to the house and won't notice that Jack is missing." Cinu smiled.

"So, that's the trick!"

Chapter Eight

THE SUPER SEVEN!

One the way, Madam Prisa saw them. She called. "Hey, where are you going?"

"We are just going to Cinu's house, ma'am." Said Muppu.

"Why?" madam Prisa asked.

"Ma'am, I forgot to take my pen. We are going to take it!" said Cinu.

"OK, then, why are you, six going?"

No answer.

"Look, Cini forgot to take HER pen. Then she will go and take it! You five go back to school!" She ordered.

"OK!" Cinu said suddenly.

Other five looked at her. She murmured to them.

"Now you go! I will come back soon and then Let's work."

And Cinu ran away. Other five went back. Cinu reached her house. There, Jicky was taking rest in her dog-house. Seeing Cinu there, she stood up. She looked surprised.

"Hey-come on Jack."

She opened the wooden door of the dog house and Jicky jumped out. Jicky started licking Cinu's feet.

“OK, that’s enough, Jack! Now look! There’s an important thing!” said Cinu.

Jicky looked at her. She saw Jicky’s eyes glittering.

“A secret-I found a mysterious forest! well, don’t know if it is true. But let’s find out! And I saw a man who looked like an explorer there!

We, the super six decided to explore that forest! We need you with us my dear!” said Cinu giving her a friendly pinch.

And Cinu took the key out of the flower pot on the varandah and opened the house. She went into her room and took the pen. Then she came out and locked the door and put the key back in flower pot.

“Come on, Jackk! It’s a crazy adverntture!” Cinu ran and Jicky ran with her.

They reached the place where the way split into two. One lead to the front gate of school and the little town nearby. Second one lead to the back part of the school compound. There was another way, leading to the river. Cinu went through the second way with Jicky. She stood at the back gate. There was a tree. One week ago, she and her friends had put a rope in the bush, there.

Cinu took the rope. And she told Jicky to go through the path which was leading to the river. There was a tiny land with green bushes and two big trees.

"Jack, listen: I will come back in the evening and then let's explore. Now, until then, you have to stay silent here!" explained Cinu and Jicky looked surprised.

“My dear, please be silent. Otherwise we’ll get into trouble.” said Cinu.

“I know you will hear me!” she tied one side of the rope on Jicky, carefully. And she tied up the other end of the rope on a tree.

“Bye! stay silent here!” Cinu ran to school.

Cinu reached the classroom. There her friends were waiting for her.

“DONE!”

She said aloud and sat down on her bench. the five looked at her.

"Now we are not super six!" she smiled.

"Jicky's with us! So, Super Seven"

"Ha-we are the SUPER SEVEN!"

The friends all said aloud in joy.

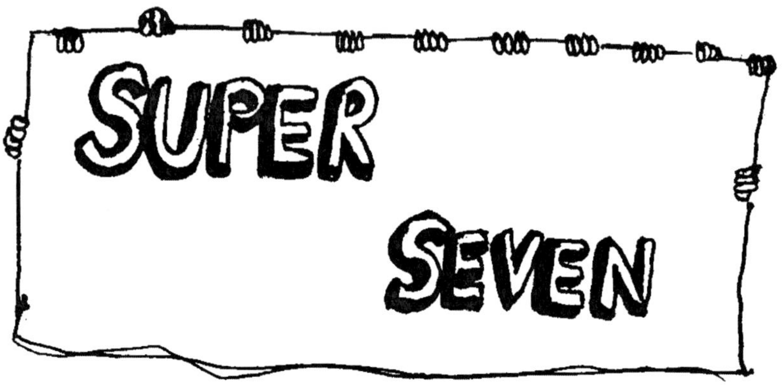

Chapter Nine

THE BIRD TRAP!

The children played many educational games. Everyone enjoyed it. Now it's evening. The teacher said.

"Ok, children! Now it's free time. Now 4 pm. You have a break until 8.30 pm OK?"

"OK!" Everyone agreed and ran out to play. Most of the children went to the ground. The six friends didn't go.

"Come with me, now" said Cinu making sure that nobody was there to over hear her.

She ran to the back gate with other five. She took them to the place where she had gone in the morning with Jicky.

There was Jicky sitting under the tree. Seeing Cinu and friends she suddenly stood up.

"Hey Jack, good girl, don't bark!" Cinu took down the rope and now Jicky was able to move as she liked.

"Jicky, be silent!" saying this, Cinu and the other six entered the school compound. Accidently Wern's sunglass fell down but they have no time to waste. The super seven moved to the mango tree area very carefully that no one would see them.

Cinu said "Go on, Jack! We'll be right behind you!"

So Jicky started walking through the mysterious wild path, sniffing. Cinu was just behind her. Arid was behind Cinu. Wern walked behind him. Aman was behind Wern. Muppu was behind him. And Oye was walking the last.

And then they reached the place where the first path ended.

"Here the second one. Let's go!" said Cinu to the excited others and they all reached inside the forest.

"This is the mysterious forest!" Cinu explained that this was where she met the stranger. After their amazement, Muppu noticed that Jicky was not there.

"Jack, Jack where are yout?" everyone called out. Suddenly Jicky appeared barking.

"I think she has found something!" said Cinu to her friends.

Jicky suddenly ran to the bushes again. So did Cinu. The other five did too. They reached a place inside the mysterious forest and saw Jicky was standing near an object with net and something on the grass.

"Yes, she found something! What is it?" children ran towards it.

"It's a BIRD TRAP!" cried Wern.

Yes, it's a bird trap! "Who had set it here?" asked Muppu.

"Another thing we have to find!" Arid said.

"Now let's go back! Let's go back before someone finds about the forest! Let's come back tomorrow!" they went back.

And Cinu went to her house with Jicky. She fed her. She put extra food and left Jicky. She came back to the school. No other person had noticed all these activities of the Super Seven.

Chapter Ten

A NEW SURPRISE!

On the next day, six friends were waiting for the evening break. At last, the free time started. Cinu went home and brought Jicky secretly and the super seven ran fast through the mysterious wild path, so excited about their adventure.

Finally, they reached the forest. It was most dark because there were black clouds covering the sun in the sky. Suddenly, Jicky looked like she was listening carefully to something. So, the children also listened.

"Ah! I can hear some footsteps do you?"

"Shh.... don't shout, be silent...."

Oye murmered as he stopped Muppu shouting aloud in excitment and fear. Of course someone's footsteps are coming near!

"Jack, don't bark!" Cinu muttered. Muppu was so scared. She was shivering.

Everyone saw a man is coming from the shadows of the trees. They were shocked. Cinu was shocked the most.

"It's him! It's HIM! Friends, I told you that

I saw a man in this forest? It's HIM! Oh, Jack, catch him! Hey-Come on guys!" she shouted aloud.

Then the man ran back. Jicky chased him; barking. And the children ran behind them. They all were going to the very dark places in the forest. Suddenly Muppu slipped and fell down.

"Aaaaaah...!"

Then her hand got a little scratch. It started bleeding and Muppu started weeping, sitting there. So, the children stopped there trying to console her.

"Jack, come back! Don't leave us here!" cried Cinu.

So, Jicky stopped running and came near to them and the man escaped.

"Don't worry, Muppu! Come on. Get-up, get up!" Muppu stood up.

"Come on look, there's a path going down! Let's go through it!"

The children and Jicky went down the way.

They reached a place that was clear with the sunlight. To their surprise, there was a small wooden house!

"Ooooohh...!"

Everyone was surprised and Muppu forgot all about her tears.

They ran towards it. "Let's check what's there inside!" Muppu ran to the door. But the door was closed and locked.

"Let's break the door!."

They took a few steps back.

"One, two, threeee.....!"

The six children and the dog ran as fast as they could towards the door and jumped on it pushing and punching it with their strength. But nothing happened to the door.

"What will we do now?" asked Oye in great disappoinment.

They all sat down on the grass.

"Jack, find out a solution!"

Cinu looked at Jicky. Then Jicky started sniffing everywhere. She stopped near the bushes and barked. Cinu ran to it. There was a key hidden there, of course; a KEY! Cinu took it up in her hands and cried.

"Hurray... we got the key...!"

Chapter Eleven

THE MAP!

Crack......! The door opened. Everyone entered the wooden house.

"What's this? What's that?"

The children were busy. They were checking everywhere. It was a small hut which had only one room. Then Aman took up a paper from the floor.

"What is this? Ooh! This is a MAP!" he cried out.

"Where-where?" others ran to see.

"This-this is wonderful!" Cinu jumped up.

Everyone looked at her.

"This means somebody had come here days or weeks or months or years ago. And there is something; that place is marked in this map!" she was too excited.

Suddenly they heard a voice.

"What is it?" asked Muppu.

Suddenly Jicky started to bark.

"Don't bark, don't bark!" Cinu stopped her.

"It's a cat!" said Arid.

"Yes! It's a cat!" others nodded.

They saw a black cat coming out of a big basket-which had a tiny cat-bed in it hidden under a table. The cat looked like she just wokeup from a great sleep right then.

"Oh!" everyone was surprised again.

Suddenly Wern jumped to the cat, before anyone could realise what was happening. They saw Wern take the cat in his hands.

"Here, this cat has a belt on her neck! Here is something written on it. W,E,R,A,L,I,A - WERALIA! May be this cat's name is

Weralia...!" he said.

Then Weralia tried to bite him and he let her go and she ran out of the house.

"Let's go back!" Muppu said.

"Yes, Jicky, you have to stay in this hut!. I have some snacks! Bye!"

Cinu put down some snacks out of her pockets and she ran out with the other five. Cinu locked the house. They looked at the house. Cinu took the key. They ran back to the school.

Chapter Twelve

WITH THE MAP!

"Come on, come on guys!" Cinu called out aloud.

It was the evening break.

"Did you take the map?" asked Oye.

"Yes, now come!"

She hurried, showing them the map in her hand. The six went into the forest. First, through the mysterious wild path. Second, through the tiny wild path. Third, in the dark zone. They were trapped!

They didn't know where to go now.

"Oops! Where's that way down?"

"Don't know!"

They lost their way in the darkest zone of the forest!

"What will we do now?"

"Jicky! Aman jumped up with the idea."

"Call your dog, call your, I mean our dog."

Everyone said to Cinu. She called out making the highest sound she could.

"Jicky... Jack...! Jaaaaaack...! Hey Jickyee....! Jack WHERE ARE YOU? JICKY..?"

She called and called and they waited and waited.

"JACK..."

Suddenly they heard a dog bark.

"JICKY, OK KEEP BARKING! BARK AGAIN AND AGAIN!" Cinu cried.

So the children were able to hear Jicky barking continuously.

"I guess it's coming from the left side. So, let's go to left!" said Arid.

So, the six children ran to left side. The barks were coming nearer. Finally they found that way down...

"Oh.... thanks to Jicky!"

They all ran down and got out of the

darkness and reached the wooden hut.

They unlocked the door and went in. There, Jicky was still barking. "Dear, you saved us!" Cinu hugged her. Then Jicky stopped barking and started licking her cheeks.

"Let's go now. Everyone; come out!"

They seven went out and Cinu pulled out the map.

"We have to go straight to the right!"

"Cinu!" Muppu suddenly hold Cinu's hand worryly.

"If there's any danger waiting for us?"

"We don't care, Muppu! Even if there is anything waiting for us, we must go! We started this adventure, so we have to end this, too."

Cinu consoled her. The super seven went to the right and jumped down the rocks as shown in the map. Now, they were on the bank of a lovely little stream. It was really little with cold water. They crossed the stream. Now there was a big green bush in front of them.

"Let's go!"

"Jack, don't bark, ok."

"Come on! " they went into the bush.

A greeny darkness for some time... And now, there was a tent in front of them.

Chapter Thirteen

A SURPRISE IN A TRAPDOOR!

The seven went into the tent. There's a small bed on the floor.

"There's something under it!" Arid dragged the bed and everyone saw a big roll of rope!

Suddenly, Oye cried out : "Here is something. Look!"

Everyone looked at the floor he was pointing at. There's a tiny trapdoor on the floor! Then Jicky started barking. The trapdoor was not locked. The children opened it. Dark inside.

"Who will jump?"

"I will!" said Cinu.

"Be careful."

The others said in a caring voice.

"Yes, I am!"

She jumped down into the trapdoor. It was not so long.

"Torch, torch, I need a torch!" she cried because it was very very dark.

Hearing this, other five started searching in the tent. Muppu found a tiny hand torch.

"YES! I HAVE FOUND IT"

"THEN GIVE IT TO ME!" said Cinu. "Throw it!" said Oye to Muppu.

Muppu threw it down into the trapdoor.

The torch fell right in front of Cinu. She took it and turned it on. She found herself standing on the mud. It was a small room. Or it looked like it is. It was empty. But there was a paper.

"Oh...! A new MAP?"

Cinu took it and looked at it. Of course, It was a map!

"Woo-Hoo..." she jumped.

"What's there? " asked the others from up in the tent.

"Let me show you! But now send me a rope!" said Cinu. So they took the rope. They held one end of it tightly and threw the other end into the trapdoor. Cinu held it. She climbed up and reached the tent.

"What have you found?" asked Wern.

"A new MAP!"

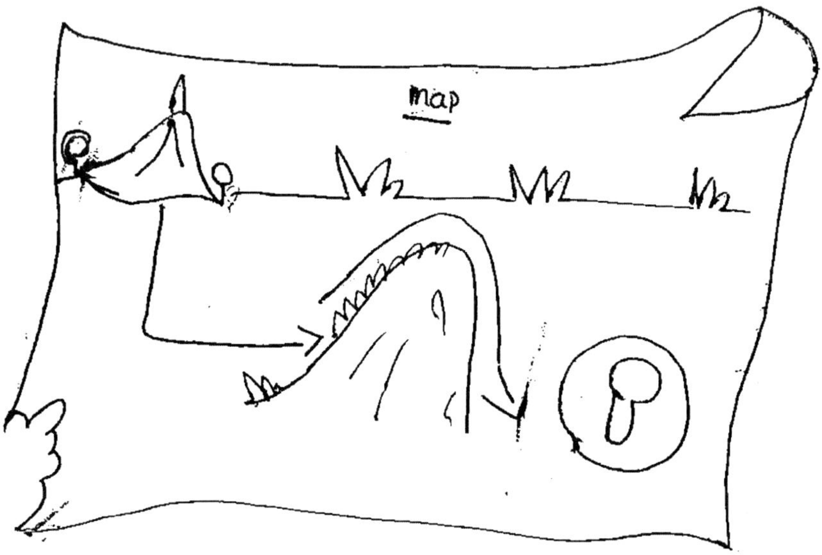

Chapter Fourteen

SOLVING THE MYSTERIES!

A cold wind was blowing. Cinu, Arid, Wern, Muppu, Aman and Oye were standing in front of another tent. Jicky was sniffing and sniffing everywhere. They reached that place following the pictures on the map. The tent was bigger than the first one.

"You stand here, Jack!" said Cinu.

So Jicky did. Then the children tried to get into the tent. Then they peeped through a window hole and saw eight men sitting inside! They were sitting in a circle.

There was a green bush nearby.

"Let's hear what they are talking." said Cinu.

Then all seven hid themselves in the bush silently. They started talking, the men in the tent.

"Ebon, why didn't Jim come?"

"I don't know, Sam! He is really worried about that incident!"

"Which incident?"

"You know it! Don't be foolish!"

"No seriously! Which incident?"

"I am saying it again! Fedwig, don't act like a fool!"

"Ha, ha! Sam, Fedwig is not acting! He is really foolish!"

"STOP IT, TOCK! I know which incident it is! We sent him to the bird trap, we had settled, to look if any birds were trapped! And then he saw a little girl there! She escaped! He was afraid that she would find that we are kidnappers, and we are getting ready to kidnap some children in that school to ask their parents, lakhs to get them back. So Jim informed us on the phone. So we escaped, came here and set up this tent..."

"STOP IT!"

"Ok all right, Bizawen-I mean sir!"

"Mmmm...!"

"Oh..! Jim is trapped. He told me that his phone is old and has problems, before he was going. I think it's damaged and has become useless, that he can't contact us! Poor Jim."

"What? So you didn't draw maps for him, Rig?"

"Yes, When...!"

"OK, now enough! Everyone sleep! Let's go to the wooden hut in the midnight and check if Jim is there."

"OK sir, let's sleep."

- Silence -

***

After a long run, super seven were now in the wooden house.

"I realized everything. The man, we saw is Jim. He and the other seven are kidnappers and they are planning to Kidnap someone in our school! They set-up that bird trap for an entertainment. And the seven sent Jim to look if any birds were trapped. This house is made by them. So, Jim saw me. He informed them on his phone. Then the others got scared. They forgot to take their pet Weralia with them in hurry. And they tried to contact Jim but his phone didn't work. So, they drew a map for him and locked the house and hid the key in the bushes for him and they ran away. The trapdoor in the second tent is to put the kids, whom they will kidnap. So that map is for Jim and they ran away and set-up the third tent where we saw them!" explained Cinu.

"So, Jim, came here but didn't get the map because we had taken it already. So he went back to the bird trap." said Arid.

"Let's go and catch him. I took the rope from the second tent!" said Oye.

So they all ran and reached near the bird trap. Jim was sitting there.

"Don't move! There are policemen hidden all over here! Don't move!" they shouted.

Jim was confused. Arid and Wern tied him tightly to a tree with the rope.

"Let's go, back!"

They left Jim and went back to the wooden house.

It was midnight. The super seven were hiding themselves silently behind the wooden hut.

Then the seven kidnappers came. They were surprised to see the door opened and went into the hut to check. When all got inside the children pulled out the key and locked the house. The kidnappers screamed and the super seven looked at each other.

"Now it's time! Let's go!"

Chapter Fifteen

THE FRIENDSHIP!

Super seven ran fast as they could with the help of the torch they got from the second tent. They reached the back side of the school.

There the teachers had informed the POLICE that six students were missing. And all of them were surprised to see them back with a dog! There started a flood of questions on them. They said only one thing:

"We need to talk to the police!"

The children told everything, what had happened, to the police inspector. He couldnot believe it. The children went with the police to show them where the hut was and the other things. Police arrested all the eight kidnappers. Everyone congratulated the super seven.

After; all that, when they got some time without others, in the shining moonglow, the children cheered together:

"We are the super seven FRIENDS"